EXPELLING DEMONS

EXPELLING DEMONS
By Derek Prince

© 2019 Derek Prince Ministries–International

Unless otherwise specified, all Scriptures are taken from the *New King James Version* of the Bible © 1982 by Thomas Nelson, Inc. All Scriptures marked NIV are taken from The Holy Bible, New International Version © 1978 by New York International Bible Society. All Scriptures marked NASB are taken from the New American Standard Bible © The Lockman Foundation 1960, 1962, 1963, 1971, 1973.

No part of this book may be reproduced or transmitted in any form or by any means, electronic or mechanical, including photocopying, recording, or by means of any information storage and retrieval system, without permission in writing from the publisher.

All rights reserved.

Printed in the USA.

ISBN 10: 1-892283-65-4
ISBN-13: 978-1-892283-65-8

Derek Prince Ministries
PO Box 19501
Charlotte, NC 28219-9501
WWW.DEREKPRINCE.ORG

DEREK PRINCE

EXPELLING DEMONS

AN INTRODUCTION INTO
PRACTICAL DEMONOLOGY

Today, by divine providence, the veils of convention and carnality are once again being drawn aside, and the church of Jesus Christ is being confronted by the same manifest opposition of demon power that confronted the church of the New Testament. In these circumstances, the church must again explore the resources of authority and power made available to her through the truth of Scripture, the anointing of the Holy Spirit, and the name and the blood of the Lord Jesus Christ.

― *Derek Prince*

EXPELLING DEMONS

BY DEREK PRINCE

"And these signs will follow those who believe: In My name they will cast out demons; they will speak with new tongues" (Mark 16:17 NKJV).

Here Christ joins closely together two manifestations of supernatural power which are to confirm the testimony of Christian believers. The first is the casting out of demons; the second is speaking with new tongues. Today in the church at large, we hear much about speaking with new tongues (especially as the evidence of the baptism in the Holy Spirit), but very little about the casting out of demons. How is it that these two manifestations have become so completely divorced from each other?

Actually, Christ places the casting out of demons *before* the speaking with new tongues. There is significance in this order. The intention is that people shall *first* be fully delivered from demons *before* they seek the baptism in the Spirit and the speaking with new tongues. However, through lack of discernment and understanding, this is not normally practiced in the church today. The result is that people nowadays are quite often baptized in the Holy Spirit and speak with new tongues but still need deliverance from demons after that. It is time for the church to devote prayerful, open-minded study to the subject of demonology.

The New Testament Greek word for "demon" is *daimonion*. This is the diminutive form of another Greek word, *daimon*. In Greek mythology and folklore, these words were used to describe a special class of beings to whom were attributed varying degrees of supernatural influence or power. Various cults and superstitious observances centered in these beings, and they played an important part in the daily lives of the common people.

In the King James Version the Greek word *daimonion* is often translated "devil." However, this is incorrect. The word "devil" is formed from the Greek word *diabolos*, which means literally "slanderer." In Scripture, this is normally reserved as a title of Satan himself.

Associated in the New Testament with the noun *daimonion* is the passive verb *daimonizomai*. The literal meaning of this verb is "to be demonized"—that is, to be in some way under the influence or power of demons. Thus the meaning of the verb is very general. In the King James Version this verb is usually translated by some phrase such as to be "possessed" or to be "vexed" by demons or by evil spirits. However, there are no distinctions in the original Greek text to which these various different English words correspond. Some preachers have worked out elaborate distinctions between possession, oppression or obsession by demons. However, there is nothing in the original Greek to support these distinctions.

Two other phrases normally used in this connection in the New Testament are "evil spirit" and "unclean spirit." A comparison of Revelation 16, verses 13 and 14, would seem to indicate that the two phrases "unclean spirits" and "spirits of demons" are used more or less interchangeably.

Psychology normally recognizes three main elements that are associated with the concept of personality. These three elements are: knowledge, will and emotion. It is important to see that all these three elements of personality are found in the New Testament picture of demons.

Demons possess *knowledge*. In Mark 1:24, the demon in the man in the synagogue at Capernaum said to Christ, "I know who You are—the Holy One of God!" In Acts 19:15, the evil spirit in the man at Ephesus said to the seven sons of Sceva, "Jesus I know [acknowledge], and Paul I know [know about]; but who are you?"

Demons possess *will*. In Matthew 12:44, the unclean spirit who has gone out of the man but can find no place of rest, says, "*I will* return to my house from which I came." In Luke 8:31–33, the demons in the man of Gadarenes displayed very strongly their will not to be cast into the abyss, but rather to be allowed to enter into the swine.

Demons possess *emotion*. In James 2:19 we read, "Even the demons believe—and *tremble!*"

Another fact that attests the personality of demons is their ability to *speak*. This is recorded in many passages of the New Testament. From the standpoint of psychology, we normally attribute the concept of personality to anything that is able to express its meaning in intelligible speech.

By every standard, therefore, we see that demons display all the attributes of *personality*. This is of tremendous importance. Christian believers are in no position to deal with demons successfully until they recognize that they are persons, not things. A demon is not a habit or a mental state or a psychological condition. A demon is a *person*.

One means by which the presence or activity of demons may be detected is the supernatural manifestation of the Holy Spirit called, in 1 Corinthians 12:10, "discerning of spirits." Many Christians who have been baptized in the Holy Spirit manifest some measure of this discernment, but quite often they do not fully realize the nature of this operation of the Holy Spirit, and therefore they do not make effective use of it. Discernment of this kind needs to be cultivated by regular exercise. For this reason, we read in Hebrews 5:14 of believers "who are of full age [maturity], that is, those who *by reason of use have their senses exercised to discern both good and evil.*" In the church today there are all too few believers who exhibit this mark of spiritual maturity.

If Christians are willing to exercise their spiritual senses, they will soon begin to discover that there are many different symptoms that commonly indicate the presence or activity of demons. Some of the most common of these symptoms are set forth below under two headings: first, psychological, related primarily to the inner nature and personality; second, physical, related primarily to the outward bodily appearance and condition.

I. Psychological

(a) Persistent or recurrent evil or destructive emotions or attitudes that can dominate a person, even contrary to his own will or nature: e.g., resentment, hatred, fear, envy, jealousy, pride, self-pity, tension, impatience.

(b) "Moods"—unreasonable, sudden, extreme fluctuations: e.g., from talkative exhilaration to taciturn depression.

(c) Various forms of religious error or bondage: e.g., submission to unscriptural doctrines or prohibitions, unnatural asceticism, refusal to eat normal foods, superstitious observances of all kinds, all forms of idolatry.

(d) Resorting to charms, fortune telling, astrology, mediums, etc.

(e) Enslaving habits: e.g., gluttony, alcohol, nicotine, drugs, sexual immorality or perversion of all kinds, uncontrollable unclean thoughts or looks.

(f) Blasphemy, mockery, unclean language.

(g) Persistent or violent opposition to the truth of Scripture or the work of the Holy Spirit.

II. Physical

(a) Unnatural restlessness and talkativeness; muttering.

(b) The eyes glazed or unnaturally bright and protruding or unable to focus naturally.

(c) Frothing at the mouth, fetid breath.

(d) Palpitation or unnaturally accelerated action of the heart.

(e) Shunning, recoiling from, or fighting against the power of the Holy Spirit.

In many cases, one of these symptoms alone would not be conclusive indication of demon presence or activity. But where several of these symptoms are found together, the probability of demon activity is extremely high.

In addition to these symptoms, the New Testament indicates plainly that demons are often the cause of purely physical sicknesses or infirmities. For instance, in Luke 13:11 we read of "a woman who had a *spirit of infirmity* eighteen years, and was bent over and could in no way raise herself up." As soon as this woman was delivered from this spirit of infirmity, her physical condition became completely normal. Jesus Himself described her as "a daughter of Abraham" (v. 16). That is to say, she was a true believer. There is no suggestion that she was guilty of any special sin. The power of the demon was manifested solely in her physical body.

Again, in Acts 19:12, we read concerning the ministry of Paul in Ephesus, "so that even handkerchiefs or aprons were brought from his body to the sick, and the diseases left them and the evil spirits went out of them." Here "evil spirits" and "diseases" are associated together in a way that plainly implies some kind of causal relationship between them.

The following are some common mental or physical conditions that are sometimes caused by demons: insanity, insomnia, epilepsy, fits, cramps, migraines, sinus infections, tumors, ulcers, heart disease, arthritis, paralysis, dumbness, deafness, blindness.

What are the conditions for deliverance from the destructive influence and power of demons?

The first condition is a *correct diagnosis*. In 1 Corinthians 9:26 Paul describes his ministry as follows: "Thus I fight: not as one who beats the air." Where Christians are confronted by demons but do not realize the nature of their enemies, they are like a boxer who lashes out wildly with his fists but never lands his blows upon his opponent's body. They may expend much time and energy, but they never make real "contact" with the unseen enemies who oppose them. For this reason, relatively little is accomplished.

Once the presence and activity of demons have been correctly diagnosed, there are a number of further conditions for deliverance. Some of these concern the believer who is seeking to minister deliverance; others concern the person who needs deliverance.

For the sake of convenience, we will call the believer who is ministering deliverance "the minister." The following are five important conditions that he should fulfill:

(1) The minister must recognize the authority delegated to him in the name of Jesus. Jesus Himself said, "*In My name* they will cast out demons" (Mark 16:17). Then, in Luke 10:17 we read, "The seventy returned with joy, saying, 'Lord, even the demons are subject to us *in Your name*.'" In Acts 16:18, when Paul spoke to the spirit of divination in the slave girl at Philippi, he said, "I command you *in the name of Jesus Christ* to come out of her."

(2) The minister needs the power of the Holy Spirit. In Matthew 12:28, Jesus said, "If I cast out demons *by the Spirit of God*, surely the kingdom of God has come upon you." He thus attributed His ability to cast out demons to the power of the Holy Spirit. Likewise, in Luke 4:18 He attributed to the anointing of the Holy Spirit His ability to "proclaim liberty [or deliverance] to the captives . . . to set at liberty those who are oppressed."

(3) The minister must understand and apply to each case the relevant principles of Scripture that define the conditions for forgiveness of sins and the legal basis of redemption through the blood of Jesus.

(4) The minister must often be prepared to provide both the time and place for intimate personal counseling. Generally speaking, the most unsuitable time or place is at the altar rail of a church during a public service!

(5) The minister must beware of spiritual pride in any form. He should be motivated by sincere, God-given compassion for the one who needs deliverance. In all the outreaches of the church today there is no more needy or pitiful class of persons than those who require deliverance from demons.

We may now turn to the case of the one who needs deliverance, who, for convenience, we will call "the patient." The following are some requirements for deliverance:

(1) **Humility.** The patient must, in humility, submit himself to God before he can resist the devil (see James 4:6–7).

(2) **Honesty.** This demands a full and frank acknowledgment both of the patient's condition and of any sins that may have contributed to that condition (see Psalm 32:1–5).

(3) **Confession.** The patient must specifically confess to God all known sin (see 1 John 1:9). In addition, he may also have to make confession to the one who is praying with him for deliverance. This is implied by the words of James 5:16: "Confess your trespasses *to one another*, and pray *for one another*." This speaks of confession not merely to God, but also to man. The order is first, "confess," then "pray."

(4) **Renunciation.** It is not enough to confess sin without also renouncing it. "He that covers his sins will not prosper, but whoever confesses and *forsakes* them will have mercy" (Proverbs 28:13). "Let the

wicked *forsake* his *way*, and the unrighteous man his *thoughts*; let him return to the Lord, and He will have mercy on him; and to our God, for He will abundantly pardon" (Isaiah 55:7). The sinner must forsake not only "his way" (his outward acts), but also "his thoughts" (any inward sinful leanings or desires, even though these are not expressed in outward acts). "Forsaking" must come before "mercy" and "pardon."

(5) **Forgiveness.** The one who desires forgiveness from God must first forgive his fellow men. Resentment and an unforgiving spirit are two of the commonest hindrances to deliverance. In Hebrews 12:15, we are warned against "any root of bitterness." Wherever bitterness has poisoned the heart, it must be totally removed, so that not even a root of it is left.

There is special significance in the order of words in the Lord's Prayer in Matthew 6:9–13. First, *"forgive us* our debts [or trespasses], *as we forgive* our debtors [or those who trespass against us]." That is to say, our forgiveness from God is in proportion to our forgiveness of our fellow men. Then, "*Deliver us* from the evil one." That is to say, *forgiveness* must come before *deliverance*. Without forgiveness, we have no right to deliverance.

(6) When the patient has met the above five conditions, he is then in a position to claim the promise of Joel 2:32: "Whoever calls on the name of the Lord shall be saved [or delivered]." Calling aloud upon the name of the Lord Jesus Christ normally sets in motion the process of deliverance.

It is important to realize that deliverance is normally a *process*. This process may be brief or long and drawn out, it may be intense and dramatic, or it may be quiet and scarcely perceptible. But whenever a person is delivered from a demon, there is some definite experience or reaction. Where there is no definite experience or reaction, it is questionable whether deliverance has really been effected.

In this connection, certain very simple, common sense principles apply. If there is a demon anywhere within a person, then that demon must come out. Unless the demon actually comes out, there has been no deliverance. Normally, a demon will seek to remain in hiding rather than be compelled to manifest its presence and come out.

A demon is a "spirit." The Greek word for "spirit," *pneuma*, also means "breath." A person's breath normally enters or leaves his body through his mouth or nose. The same is true of demons/evil spirits. When a demon comes out of a person, it normally comes out through his mouth. At this point, there is usually some definite manifestation. The following are some manifestations connected with the mouth that commonly mark the culmination of the process of deliverance: a hiss, a cough, sobbing, screaming, roaring, belching, spitting or vomiting.

The phenomena of screaming or roaring are referred to in Acts 8:7: "Unclean spirits, *crying with a loud voice*, came out of many who were possessed." However these are only two, out of various possible phenomena, connected in some way with the mouth. Experience has convinced me that different classes of demons exhibit different types of behavior.

For example, demons of sexual uncleanness normally come out with some form of spitting or vomiting (and quite often large amounts of slimy, mucous material are brought up in this process). The demon of fear normally comes out with a kind of hysterical sobbing or whimpering. The demons of lying and of hatred utter a load roar. The demon of nicotine (smoking) comes out with a cough or a gasp.

It sometimes happens that demons virtually set aside the personality of the patient and manifest and express their own personality through him. At times, they take control of the patient's organs of speech and use these to utter their own words. Sometimes this causes an obvious change of voice. A gruff, masculine type of voice may be heard out of a woman's throat. It sometimes happens also that the demon within a person may understand and speak a language not known by the person himself.

In such cases, the minister may exercise the authority delegated to him through the name of Jesus and may command each demon to name itself, thus revealing its nature and activity. The following are some of the names that I have heard given: Fear, Hatred, Lies, Doubt, Envy, Jealousy, Confusion, Perversity, Schizophrenia, Death, Suicide, Adultery, Mockery, Blasphemy, Witchcraft. I have also heard a number of other names that are too obscene to print.

Please note that I don't recommend talking to demons in a conversational way, but it is scriptural to ask them questions and compel them to answer.

Let me just state in closing that through my own personal life and experience, I have proved afresh the accuracy and reliability of the Scriptures. Demons are just the way they are described. They behave the same way and they need to be treated the same way—it works.

Finally, make Jesus central in your life. I have come to understand, in a new way, the significance of the cross. In the spiritual world, denominations amount to nothing. All that matters is what Christ did on the cross: His shed blood, His death, His resurrection, and what that means to the believer.

In John 12:31, Jesus said this when He went to the cross: "Now is the judgment of this world: is the prince of the world [Satan] cast out."

If Satan is cast out, then there is a vacuum that needs filled. Who is going to fill it? The next verse says: "And I [Jesus], if I be lifted up from the earth, will draw all men unto me." Make it your supreme aim to always uplift and glorify Jesus.

Prayer of Release

Lord Jesus Christ, I believe You are the Son of God and the only way to God. I believe You died on the cross for my sins and rose again from the dead. I come to You now for mercy and for forgiveness. I believe You have forgiven me. Because You have forgiven me, I am now a child of God. Now Lord, You know the special problem I have with the demonic influences that torment me. Jesus, I want to meet Your conditions and receive Your deliverance.

First of all, I forgive every person who ever harmed me or wronged me. I forgive them all now. (Now pause for a moment and name everyone you need to forgive.) Lord, I forgive all these people. I lay down all bitterness, all resentment, all hatred, and all rebellion. As I forgive them, I believe You have forgiven me. Thank You for that forgiveness.

I also renounce every contact with Satan, with occult powers, with secret societies, with anything in Satan's territory. I repent of being involved in these pursuits, and I turn my back on all those activities. Also, Lord if there is a curse over my life, I remove it now in Your name. I thank You that on the cross You were made a curse that I might be redeemed from the curse to receive the blessing. I claim that now, releasing myself from all curses and entering into the blessings of God.

Now I come against any evil spirit in me that occupies any area of my personality. I declare my hatred of these spirits — and remove them as my enemies. I will not make peace with them. I will not compromise with them. They will have no more place in me. I turn against them now. In the authority of Your name, Jesus, I command them to leave me. I expel them right now in the name of Jesus. Amen.

Begin to expel them at this time. They may go out all at once, or one at a time as you identify them. Take all the time that is necessary.

Please remember that one more step is needed to keep your deliverance. You must fill up the vacuum left by the expelled spirits with Jesus. Confirm your commitment to Jesus as the Lord of your life. He will fill up the empty spaces by the power of the Holy Spirit.

After you experience your deliverance, start to thank God and praise Him for cleansing you and filling every area of your life.

For Further Study

Audio CD or MP3

Deliverance & Demonology (6-CD series, #CDDD1)
Derek first exposes the nature and activity of demons, then explains the crucial steps to receiving deliverance and permanent freedom.

Disk 1 - *How I Came to Grips with Demons*
After preaching the "full gospel" for 20 years, I was directed by God into a "postgraduate course" on demonology and forced to reevaluate my doctrinal preconceptions. A Baptist lady and her daughter are delivered of demons and I am openly challenge by demons in my own Sunday morning worship service. This is a new phase in my ministry and brings about four important results in my life.

Disk 2 - *How Jesus Dealt with Demons*
Learn eleven important lessons from the ministry of Jesus. Healing and casting out demons were two continuing major features of Jesus' ministry. He always did this in public and combined it with the teaching of God's Word. He never sent anyone to preach without first giving him authority to cast out demons.

Disk 3 - *Nature and Activity of Demons*
Helps you distinguish between "devil" and "demons." There are three Greek expressions used

For Further Study

to describe the influence of demons—the King James Version's use of "possession" is misleading. Demons differ from fallen angels because they have all the marks of personality. I reveal six main forms of demon activity.

Disk 4 - *How to Recognize and Expel Demons*
Contains the personal testimony of deliverance from a spirit of depression. There is a "city" within each person. Learn the six main areas of the "city" with the characteristic demon occupants. Apply the six main steps to deliverance and practical instruction on how to receive deliverance.

Disk 5 - *Cult and Occult: Satan's Snares Disclosed*
Explains three main forms of Satan's bondage: (1) Domination of one person by another (frequently a form of witchcraft), (2) Heresies (i.e. departures from the Christian faith), and (3) False, non-Christian religions. Explanation of words used in KJV for occult practices and definitions of divination, witchcraft, sorcery. Modern forms of these practices prevalent today.

Disc 6 - *Seven Ways to Keep Your Deliverance*
Answers to frequently asked questions like: How do I know if I am completely free? Where do demons go? Why are some people not delivered? The seven main requirements for staying free.

For Further Study

Basics of Deliverance (2-CD series, # CDTS026)
Controversial, yet scriptural. Deliverance from demonic influence is a relevant and needed ministry in today's church. Drawing on 22 years of experience in the ministry of deliverance, Derek Prince imparts the basic truths that bring freedom.

Disc 1 - *How to Identify the Enemy*
How to identify the enemy based on the pattern of Jesus' ministry. The equipping of disciples. The nature of demons, evil, or unclean spirits, and their characteristics. What your objectives should be and how to distinguish between flesh and demons.

Disc 2 - *How to Expel the Enemy*
How demons get in. How to be delivered. Explaining why some are not delivered. How to keep your deliverance.

How to Be Delivered (CD or DVD, #4398)
Deliverance from evil spirits is the one miracle that has no counterpart in the Old Testament. It is, therefore, the one distinctive sign that the Kingdom of God has come.

Instruction on Deliverance for Children and Their Parents (CD or MP3, #CD6008)
Teaching parents, who are responsible to God for the spiritual well-being of their children, how to deliver and protect their family from evil spirits.

For Further Study

Books

They Shall Expell Demons (#B42)

Jesus never sent anyone out to preach the Gospel without specifically instructing and equipping them to take action against demons in the same way that He Himself did. (254 pages, 5.5 x 8.5 in.)

Protection from Deception (#B94)

Navigating through the minefield of signs and wonders. In the midst of confusion and deception, God's Word provides a clear path on which to walk in peace and safety. (240 pages, 6 x 9 in.)

Blessing or Curse: You Can Choose! (#B56)

Are you continually frustrated by sickness, financial pressure, strained relationships or other struggles that just won't go away? (295 pages, 5.5 x 8.5 in.)

About the Author

Derek Prince (1915–2003) was born in Bangalore, India of British parents. Educated as a scholar of Greek and Latin at Eton College, and King's College, Cambridge University, England, where he held a Fellowship in Ancient and Modern Philosophy. He studied several modern languages, including Hebrew and Aramaic, at Cambridge University and the Hebrew University in Jerusalem.

While serving with the British army in World War II, he began to study the Bible and experienced a life-changing encounter with Jesus Christ. Out of this encounter he formed two conclusions: first, that Jesus Christ is alive; second, that the Bible is a true, relevant, up-to-date book. These conclusions altered the whole course of his life, which he then devoted to studying and teaching the Bible.

Derek's main gift of explaining the Bible and its

teaching in a clear and simple way has helped build a foundation of faith in millions of lives. His non-denominational, non-sectarian approach has made his teaching equally relevant and helpful to people from all racial and religious backgrounds.

He is the author of over 100 books, 600 audio and 110 video teachings, many of which have been translated and published in more than 100 languages. His daily radio broadcast is translated into Arabic, Bahasa (Indonesia), Chinese (Amoy, Cantonese, Mandarin, Shanghaiese, Swatow), Croatian, German, Malagasy, Mongolian, Russian, Samoan, Spanish, and Tongan. The radio program continues to touch lives around the world.

Derek Prince Ministries continues to reach out to believers in over 140 countries with Derek's teachings, fulfilling the mandate to keep on "until Jesus returns." Outreach offices are around the world, including primary work in Australia, Canada, China, France, Germany, the Netherlands, New Zealand, Norway, Russia, South Africa, Switzerland, the United Kingdom and the United States. For current information about these and other worldwide locations, visit: www.derekprince.org.

Derek Prince Ministries Offices Worldwide

Albania	Myanmar
Armenia	Nepal
Australia	Netherlands
Bosnia-Herzegovina	New Zealand
Bulgaria	Norway
Cambodia	Papua New Guinea
Canada	Philippines
China	Poland
Croatia	Romania
Czech Republic	Russia
Denmark	Serbia
Egypt	Singapore
Estonia	Slovakia
Ethiopia	Slovenia
France	Solomon Islands
Germany	South Africa
Ghana	Sri Lanka
Hungary	Sweden
India	Switzerland
Indonesia	Uganda
Israel	Ukraine
Japan	United Kingdom
Kenya	United States
Malaysia	Zimbabwe

Connect with us

facebook.com/dpmlegacy

youtube.com/DerekPrinceMinistry

twitter.com/DPMUSA

instagram.com/derek_prince_usa/

pinterest.com/derekprinceusa

download our app in your app store

WWW.DEREKPRINCE.ORG